Journey of a Bowl of Cornflakes

John Malam

Heinemann
LIBRARY

Chicago, Illinois

www.capstonepub.com
Visit our website to find out more information about Heinemann-Raintree books.

To order:

☎ Phone 800-747-4992

💻 Visit www.capstonepub.com
to browse our catalog and order online.

Edited by Dan Nunn and Diyan Leake
Designed by Cynthia Della-Rovere
Original illustrations © Capstone Global Library Ltd 2013
Illustrated by Capstone Global Library Ltd
Picture research by Mica Brancic
Production by Alison Parsons

Originated by Capstone Global Library Ltd
Printed and bound in China by Leo Paper Products Ltd

16 15 14 13 12
10 9 8 7 6 5 4 3 2 1

Cataloging-in-Publication Data is available at the Library of Congress website.

ISBN: 978-1-4329-6601-0 (HB)
ISBN: 978-1-4329-6608-9 (PB)

Acknowledgments
The author and publishers are grateful to the following for permission to reproduce copyright material: Alamy pp. 16 (© Jeff Greenberg), 21 (© sciencephotos), 25 (© Art Directors & TRIP); © Capstone Publishers pp. 18 (Karon Dubke), 27 (Karon Dubke); Corbis pp. 20 (© Peter Yates), 28 (© the food passionates); © Dusko Matic pp. 15, 19; Getty Images pp. 12 (© Aurora/Tom Sperduto), 22 (© Dmitry Kalinovsky), 23 (© Photodisc/ Monty Rakusen); © Kellogg's p. 14; Science Photo Library p. 26 (© Peter Menzel); Shutterstock pp. 3 (© Picsfive), 4 (© Brooke Becker), 5 (oats, © Sinelyov), 5 (corn, © Giuseppe R), 5 (rice, © Imageman), 5 (wheat, © Imageman), 6 (© Tom Fakler), 7 (© Bandy), 9 (© Foto011), 10 (© Steve Heap), 11 (© Tish1), 13 (© Africa Studio), 17 (© Picsfive), 24 (© Eric Gevaert), 29 top (© Giuseppe R), 29 bottom (© Brooke Becker), 31 top (© Foto011), 31 middle (© Africa Studio), 31 bottom (© Picsfive).

Cover photographs of a corn field (© Tish1) and a bowl of cornflakes (© Oliver Hoffmann) reproduced with permission of Shutterstock.

Every effort has been made to contact copyright holders of material reproduced in this book. Any omissions will be rectified in subsequent printings if notice is given to the publisher.

Disclaimer
All the Internet addresses (URLs) given in this book were valid at the time of going to press. However, due to the dynamic nature of the Internet, some addresses may have changed, or sites may have changed or ceased to exist since publication. While the author and publisher regret any inconvenience this may cause readers, no responsibility for any such changes can be accepted by either the author or the publisher.

Contents

Some words are shown in bold, **like this**. You can find out what they mean by looking in the Glossary.

What's for Breakfast?

Breakfast is the first meal of the day. You eat breakfast in the morning, soon after you wake up. Breakfast gives your body the energy it needs for a good start to the day.

Does your breakfast cereal look like one of these?

corn

rice

oats

wheat

Many people eat **cereal** for breakfast. Most breakfast cereals are made from the **grains** of plants such as wheat, oats, rice, and corn.

Corn to Cornflake

Cornflakes are one type of breakfast **cereal**. They are made from **grains** of a plant called corn. Corn is sometimes also called **maize**.

The part that the corn grains grow on is called an ear.

Cornflakes start off as soft grains of corn growing in farmers' fields. They end up as crunchy cereal that people eat with milk for breakfast.

Growing the Corn

Corn grows in many countries. Most corn grows in the United States. Farmers **sow** their fields with corn seeds every year.

U.S. "Corn Belt" state

This map shows the areas where corn grows in the United States.

CANADA

Minnesota

Michigan

South Dakota

Wisconsin

Iowa

Nebraska

Illinois

Ohio

Indiana

Kansas

Missouri

UNITED STATES

ATLANTIC OCEAN

MEXICO

North

West — East

South

0   150   300 miles
0   150   300 kilometers

8

Corn seeds grow into tall plants.

Each plant has one or two ears of corn. There are hundreds of soft, juicy **grains** or **kernels** of yellow corn on each ear.

Harvesting the Corn

The sun warms the ears of corn. The **kernels** become hard and dry. Farmers **harvest** the sun-dried corn kernels in September. Only the best kernels are used for cornflakes.

This farmer is harvesting a field of corn.

A combine harvester is a big machine.

Some farmers drive a combine harvester through the fields of corn. The combine cuts the ears off the corn plants. Then, it takes the kernels off the ears.

From Farm to Mill

Farmers sell the dried **kernels** to a corn **mill**. Trucks take the kernels from the farm to the mill. At the mill, the kernels are cleaned and sorted.

This farmer is unloading his corn harvest so that it is ready to take to a corn mill.

Each grit
of corn will
become a
cornflake.

When the kernels are clean, they go into a
milling or grinding machine. It breaks them
into small, hard pieces called **grits**.

From Mill to Factory

The corn **mill** sells the corn **grits** to a cornflake **factory**. At the factory, the hard grits are put into a **steam** cooker for about one hour. Then, the grits are dried in a machine.

There are many big buildings at a cornflake factory.

The grits have changed shape and become flakes.

The dried grits go to a machine that squeezes them between two large rollers. When they come out of the rolling machine, they look like cornflakes for the first time.

Toasting the Flakes

The flakes of corn are still very soft when they leave the rolling machine. They are toasted inside a big oven to turn them into crunchy cornflakes. Thousands of flakes of corn are tossed around inside the oven.

There are switches to control the machines in the cornflake **factory**.

These are freshly toasted cornflakes, straight from the oven.

The oven is very hot. It is much hotter than an oven at home. It only takes a few seconds to toast the flakes. The oven makes them crisp and turns them a golden-brown color.

Adding Flavor

A **conveyor belt** takes the toasted cornflakes to a big drum. Inside the drum, the cornflakes are sprayed all over with sugar, flavors, **vitamins**, and **minerals**.

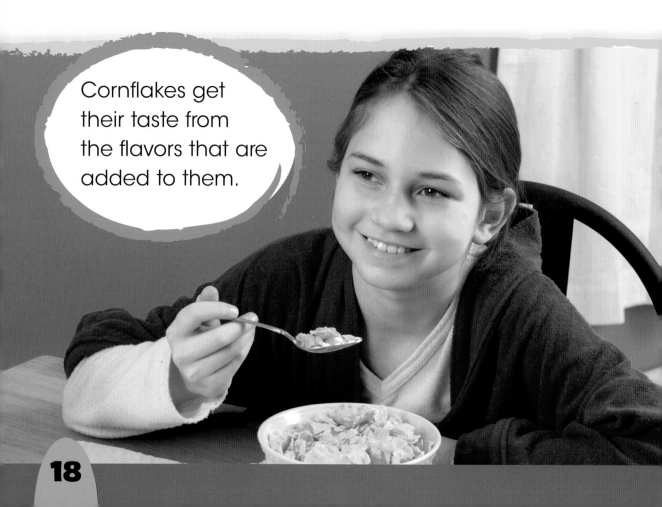

Cornflakes get their taste from the flavors that are added to them.

Another conveyor belt takes the cornflakes to the bagging area. A machine weighs the right amount of cornflakes for each bag. The cornflakes drop into a bag. The top of the bag is sealed. It takes just two seconds to fill a bag with cornflakes and seal it.

Into Boxes

The filled cornflake bags move to a packing machine. This puts them into boxes. The boxes are made out of thin cardboard and have the **brand** of the cornflakes on them. There are lots of different brands of cornflakes.

The boxes leave the packing machine when they are full of cornflakes.

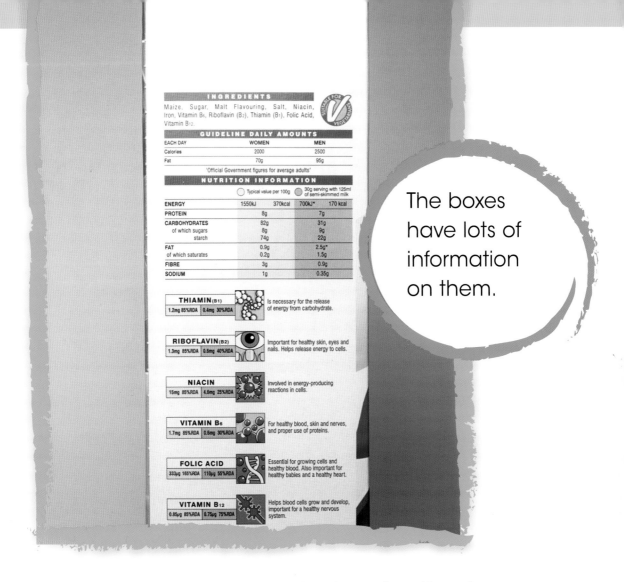

The boxes have lots of information on them.

Each brand has its own design for the box. There is information about the **ingredients** in the cornflakes. There is a "Best Before" date. It means that it is best to eat the cornflakes before that date.

In the Warehouse

The boxes of cornflakes are packed into large cardboard cartons. Each carton holds lots of boxes. The cartons are sent to a **warehouse**.

There are lots of shelves in a warehouse.

This truck is being loaded with cartons of cornflakes.

The cartons of cornflakes are stacked on high shelves in the warehouse. Trucks go to the warehouse and pick them up. The cornflakes are loaded onto the trucks.

On the Road

The trucks may have to go a long way. They drive to supermarkets and other stores.

These trucks have arrived at a big supermarket.

The boxes of cornflakes need to be stacked carefully.

The cartons of cornflakes are unloaded and opened. People working at the supermarket put the boxes of cornflakes onto the shelves.

At the Supermarket

Shoppers choose which **brand** of cornflakes they want. There are lots to choose from! There are also other **cereals** made from other **grains**.

Shoppers take the box of cornflakes to the checkout line along with their other items. They pay for it and take it home.

Just Add Milk!

At breakfast, you put some cornflakes into a bowl. Pour fresh milk over them and they are ready to eat.

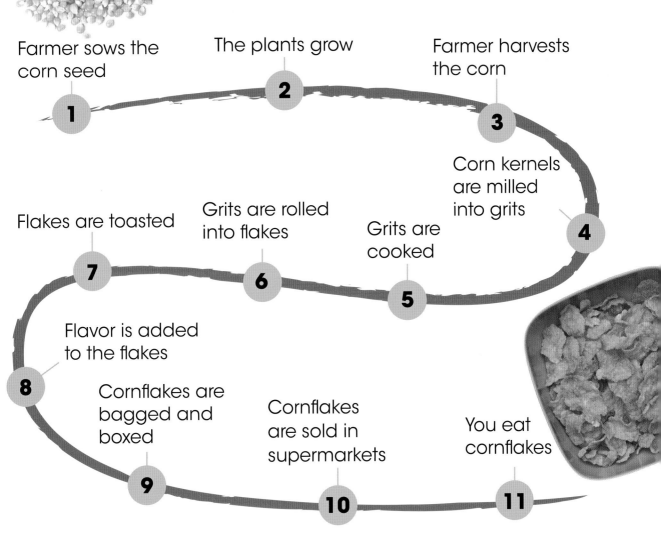

Farmer sows the corn seed **1**

The plants grow **2**

Farmer harvests the corn **3**

Corn kernels are milled into grits **4**

Grits are cooked **5**

Grits are rolled into flakes **6**

Flakes are toasted **7**

Flavor is added to the flakes **8**

Cornflakes are bagged and boxed **9**

Cornflakes are sold in supermarkets **10**

You eat cornflakes **11**

From start to finish, it takes between six and eight months to make cornflakes. Somewhere in the world, a farmer is growing corn right now. That corn may become the cornflakes that you eat in a few months.

Glossary

brand name of a particular make of goods

cereal breakfast food made from grains

conveyor belt rubber surface that moves along, carrying things on it

factory building where things are made

grain small, hard seed of a cereal plant

grit broken-up piece of corn grains

harvest gather in the crops

ingredient part used in a mixture; one of the foods in a recipe

kernel single whole grain of corn

maize another word for corn

mill factory where corn grains are prepared

mineral something found in meat, beans, and other foods, which the human body needs to stay healthy

sow plant a seed

steam water that is in the form of a gas, because it is very hot

vitamin something found in fruits, vegetables, and other foods, which the human body needs to stay healthy

warehouse building where things are stored

Cornflake Quiz

1. What plants do the kernels used in cornflakes grow on? (See page 6.)

2. What color are corn kernels? (See page 9.)

3. What are corn kernels broken down into? (See page 13.)

4. How long does it take to toast cornflakes? (See page 17.)

5. What do you pour over cornflakes during breakfast? (See page 28.)

Find Out More

This video explains how cereals like cornflakes are made:
www.youtube.com/watch?v=pJ6ek9UOvxA

Here is an animated guide to corn and its uses:
urbanext.illinois.edu/corn/03.html

Answers

1. corn plants, 2. yellow, 3. grits, 4. a few seconds, 5. milk

Index